Bantam

JACKIE KAY was born in Edinburgh. She is the third
modern Makar, the Scottish poet laureate. A poet, novelist
and writer of short stories, she has enjoyed great acclaim for
her work for both adults and children. Her first novel, *Trumpet*,
won the Authors' Club First Novel Award and the Guardian
Fiction Prize. She is also the author of three collections of stories
for Picador, *Why Don't You Stop Talking*, *Wish I Was Here*,
and *Reality, Reality*; a poetry collection, *Fiere*; and her memoir,
Red Dust Road. She is Professor of Creative Writing at
Newcastle University, and divides her time between
Glasgow and Manchester, where she is currently
Chancellor of the University of Salford.

Jackie Kay

Bantam

PICADOR

First published 2017 by Picador
an imprint of Pan Macmillan
20 New Wharf Road, London N1 9RR
Associated companies throughout the world
www.panmacmillan.com

ISBN 978-1-5098-6317-4

ACKNOWLEDGEMENTS
Zora Neale Hurston, *Moses, Man of the Mountain* (Harper Perennial)
Hugh MacDiarmid, *The Selected Poems of Hugh MacDiarmid* (Penguin)
Rupert Brooke, *The Collected Poems of Rupert Brooke* (John Lane)
Nan Shepherd, *The Living Mountain* (Canons)

1 3 5 7 9 8 6 4 2

A CIP catalogue record for this book is available from the British Library.

Printed and bound by CPI Group (UK) Ltd, Croydon, CR0 4YY

Visit **www.picador.com** to read more about all our books
and to buy them. You will also find features, author interviews and
news of any author events, and you can sign up for e-newsletters
so that you're always first to hear about our new releases.

The present was an egg laid by the past that
had the future inside its shell
Zora Neale Hurston

My clan is darkness 'yont a wee ring
O' memory showin' catsiller herc or there
But nocht complete or lookin' twice the same
Hugh MacDiarmid

These hearts were woven of human joys and cares,
Washed marvellously with sorrow, swift to mirth.
The years had given them kindness. Dawn was theirs,
And sunset, and the colours of the earth.
Rupert Brooke

It's a grand thing to get leave to live
Nan Shepherd

For Matthew Kay
With love

Contents

Lines for Kilmarnock

(for the new war memorial in Kilmarnock)

Between the lines of men,
The lines of women come:

In case you think me strange,
Your postscript never came.

The lines you repeat before you fall
Into line, and the ones you say when you fall

Asleep. Dear John, dear, dear, darling –
Lines unsaid, lines unformed.

You were a line crossed out, erased.
Dazed, the girl who waits late, frazzled, fazed.

The living still had to write a line. Messages:
Poached rabbit. Out of your mind!

Then the soup line; and on the bread line –
There again – two eagles flown to the wind.

How you were left behind, left behind,
To feed the mumbling mouths of weans.

Family lines:
Broken. I won't carry a gun, he said.

I will carry the wounded, he said.
And for years, she did, she took the dead on her back.

I listened to you in my dreams, you said. Knock, Knock.
I'm sending a kiss from Kilmarnock.

Years down the line, there are the lines
You'll have said to the dead, who, all of a sudden,

Return and keep returning like the blossom to the trees,
Like the wintergreen along the borderlines.

Return now to walk this fine line between the living
And the dead, winter or spring, winter or spring.

Bantam

(My father at 87 remembers his father at 17)

It wisnae men they sent tae war
It wis boys like the Bantams
– wee men named efter
sma' chickens,
or later a jeep, a bike, a camera.
That needy, fir soldiers, they drapped height
Restriction, so small men came to war.
As a prisoner, my faither's weight dropped
And years later, the shrapnel frae the Somme
Shot oot, a wee jewel hidden in his right airm.

Private Joseph Kay

My grandfather, Joseph Kay, Highland Light Infantry —
After his capture on the 17th of January,

Prisoner of war, Bourlon, Cambrai, and on and on
From the Second Battle of the Somme,

After the death of friends who did not become
Fathers, grandfathers, husbands, old sons,

Tram drivers, shipbuilders, miners,
Lovers, joiny-inners — never, ever raised his voice in anger.

My father, John Kay, boy, up at dawn,
Spies his father (shy man, bit withdrawn, shrapnel in his arm)

Polishing the brass buttons of his tram driver's uniform,
(Heavy, green)

In a slot-like machine,
The smell of Woodbine, shoes shined, his voice rising

Coorie doon, coorie doon, coorie doon my darling
Lie doon my dear and in your ear

What was that Wagner aria?
Song sheets flutter. Blood, bone, air,

Ballads slide down the years, broken lines.
My father, ninety, still singing his father

There's life in the old dog yet, John pipes
Private Joseph Kay takes a long breath,

Hits the note, hangs on, blows out.

Vault

(after Marion Coutts, For the Fallen)

And just when we thought, when we thought, when we thought
          We could not   we could not
          We did, we did   we leapt, we leapt
          We made it   across, across.
          We fell often   were broken; we lost.
        The past is a leap   in the dark: a dark horse.
         We laughed. We wept. Of course, of course.

By Accident

'It hurt. It hurt like hell. But it didn't matter, if no one knew.'
Nella Larsen, Passing

There is no answer for a broken heart, she said.
Now I can't forget the way she held her head up high.
She was always kind, my Mama, dignified.
There's nothing as potent as regret, I said, out loud,
Though she's gone to the big upland in the sky,
And the band is playing jazz, I hope, playing it loud.
If ever you pass me in the street, pass me by, I said.
I was too busy being somebody else, telling lies,
Too full of shame of kindred, blood and line.
I should've shut my mouth, not averted my eye.
How I wish she could un-die, my kith, my kin.
The hands of time were pearly white, you see.
If you want to blame somebody, don't blame me!
If I loved her too much, I'm sorry, she said.

A Lang Promise

Whether the weather be dreich or fair, my luve,
if guid times greet us, or we hae tae face the worst,
ahint and afore whit will happen tae us:
blind in the present, eyes open to the furore,
unkempt or perjink, suddenly puir or poorly,
peely-wally or in fine fettle, beld or frosty,
calm as a ghoul or in a feery-farry,
in dork December or in springy spring weather,
doon by the Barrows, on the Champs-Élysées,
at midnicht, first licht, whether the mune
be roond or crescent, and yer o' soond mind
or absent, I'll tak your trusty haun
and lead you over the haw – hame, ma darlin.
I'll carry ma lantern, and daur defend ye agin ony foe;
and whilst there is breath in me, I'll blaw it intae ye.
Fir ye are ma true luve, the bonnie face I see;
nichts I fall intae slumber, it's ye swimming up
in all yer guidness and blitheness, yer passion.
You'll be mine, noo, an' till the end o' time,
ma bonnie lassie, I'll tak the full guid o' ye'
and gie it back, and gie it back tae ye:
a furst kiss, a lang promise, time's gowden ring.

Diamond Colonsay

What joy to see love endure, dears,
To come down the stairs at Glassard
To overhear *I love you John Kay*
I love you Helen Kay.

Like a surprise honeymoon, Colonsay,
The shimmering sea, the long day
The frank moon, the stars, the Milky Way.
How the years slide away.

The seals slither off rocks to the bay.
You sing every day to each other
A ballad, blues or bawdy number
Love: naturally occurs. Hardy.

Comrades, compadres, companions,
Love on the rise of the lapwing's wing
Up the hill and round the bend, singing,
Sixty years of ding-dong.

Past the golden sands of Kiloran Bay,
The big woods, the Aspen Well
Over the cairns of Cnoc Beag
Love: a hut circle, standing stones.

Find it in the kitchen for a wee dance,
In the back of the car through the crags and duns

Love: climbing the MacPhees in one day,
Give it a new word, this diamond, dear ones

Call it Colonsay, the call of Colonsay!
Helen and John, John and Helen Kay.

April Sunshine

When the people who have lived all their lives,
For democracy, for democracy,
Survive to see the spring, April sunshine,
It's a blessing; it's a blessing.

In the hospital this bleak mid-winter,
You were just an old woman;
You were just an old man.

Nobody imagined how you marched against Polaris,
How you sat down at Dunoon – stood up for U.C.S.
Nobody pictured you writing to Mandela
And fifty other prisoners of South Africa.

You were just an old woman;
You were just an old man.

Nobody knew you greeted Madame Allende
Or sang the songs of Victor Jara
Or loved Big Arthur's bravura 'Bandiera Rossa'
Or heard Paul Robeson at the May Day rally

You were just an old woman;
You were just an old man.

And how just last Saturday you were mad
You couldn't march against Trident with Nicola Sturgeon.

You say: *One less missile would subsidize the arts for a century!*
You say: *Which politician will stand up for the refugees!*

You would have struggled there with your new grey stick!
You would have walked with your poppy red Zimmer.
What do we want? You say! *Peace in society.*
Time has not made your politics dimmer.

When the people who lived all their lives
For democracy, for democracy,
Survive to see the springtime, April sunshine,
It's a blessing; it's a blessing.

Rannoch Loop

Back here, the iron line crosses future, past:
Then my father will surely be seen

Trekking the sodden, lonely land,
Weekenders, together –

Or trudging through the ancient pine woods,
The musk smell of red deer,

My father, here on the moor,
Years and years after he's gone,

Held by the land's callused hands.
Och – big hikes across time, lochs, bogs,

September weekend or Easter, far flung,
Doon by Loch Ericht, on the west side

To the old crofter's burnt-out croft,
Still a magnificent doss, and he'll doss there,

(Twelve men to the wee hoose)
And rest, rest, till finally refreshed.

Rannoch Moor, Rannoch dear.
Beloved best, the best: back here.

Small

(i.m. Roanne Dods)

It's always the small that
gets you, a wee act
of kindness, the tiniest detail,
a stranger's caress,
your heart, the way you react
when faced with the trials.
The gift of a bluebell, an embrace,
Oh – the yellow gorse,
the small brown foals,
the crows lined up
from the train window.
Beauty, inches close to sorrow.

Threshold

Let's hae a blether about doors.
Revolving doors and sliding doors;

Half-opened, half-closed:
The door with your name on it,

The heavy one — hard to open.
The one you walked out when your heart was broken,

The one you went through in your new profession
(And the tiny one when you made your first confession)

The school door at the end of a lesson,
(Shut the door in Gaelic is duin an doras!)

The wee door on your doll's house, or
Ibsen's Nora's door, or Chekhov's Three Sisters:

Or Chris Guthrie's open heart at the end of *Sunset Song*
Or the step left when the house is gone, the haw.

The door to the stable, bolted too late
Not Tam O'Shanter's tail-less horse!

The one that shut suddenly behind you
Banged by a violent wind,

The painted red for asylum seeker,
The X that says Plague or Passover

The one turned into a boat to cross the waters.
The North Sea and the Aegean, reminders

Of the people cleared off their land, out their crofts
To whom the sea was their threshold – on, off.

Take the big key and open the door to the breathing past
The one you enliven over and over,

To the ship's port, the house of the welder,
The library door of Donald Dewar.

Then picture yourself on the threshold,
The exact moment when you might begin again,

Come through to this Parliament, new session!
Pass round the revolving door

Here – rising out of the slope of Arthur's Seat
Straight into this City, a city that must also speak

For Munros, cairns, bothies
The banks and braes, the stories,

(And don't forget the ceilidhs – who disnae love a ceilidh? Heuch!)
A city that remembers the fiddlers of Shetland and Orkney

The folk of Colonsay, Bute and Tiree
The Inner and Outer Hebrides, the glens and the Bens

The trees and the rivers and the burns
And the lochs and the sea lochs (and Nessie!)

The Granite City and Dumfries and Galloway
The Dear Green Place and Maw Broon's Dundee . . .

Across the stars and the galaxy,
The night sky's tiny keys, the hail clanjamfrie!

Find here what you are looking for:
Democracy: guard her

Like you would a small daughter
And keep the door wide open, not just ajar,

And say, in any language you please,
Welcome, welcome to the world's refugees.

Scotland's changing faces – look at me!!
Whose birth mother came through the door

Of a mother and baby home here
And walked out of Elsie Inglis Hospital alone.

My Makar, her daughter, Makar
Of Ferlie Leed and gallus tongues.

*   *   *

[17]

And this is my country says the fisherwoman from Jura.
Mine too says the child from Canna and Iona.

Mine too say the Brain family.
And mine! says the man from the Polish deli

And mine said the brave and beautiful Asad Shah.
Me too said the Black Scots and the red Scots

Said William Wallace and Mary Queen of Scots,
Said both the Roberts and Muriel Spark,

Said Emeli Sandé and Arthur Wharton,
Said Ali Smith and Edwin Morgan,

Said Liz Lochhead, Norman and Sorley.
And mine, said the Syrian refugee.

Here we are, in this building of pure poetry
On this July morning in front of her Majesty.

Good Day Ma'am, Ma'am Good Day.
Good morning John and Helen Kay –

Great believers in democracy,
And in giein it laldy.

Our strength is our difference.
Dinny fear it. Dinny caw canny.

It takes more than one language to tell a story,
欢迎
Gbɛgbɔgblɔ ɖeka sese menyo tututu o
Witamy
एक कहानी सुनाने के लिए, एक से अधिक भाषाएं लगती हैं
Lleva màs de un idioma contar una historia,
ਸਵਾਗਤ ਹੈ
Une seule langue n'est jamais suffisante
Hadithimoja ni kamwe ya kutosha.
Tervetuloa
Fàilte
It takes mair nor ae tongue tae crack
أهلاً بك
Nnọọ!
Benvingudes.
O singură limbă nu este niciodată de ajuns.
herzlich willkommen
Jedan jezik nikad nije dovoljno.
Üdvözlégy.
Välkomna
Vitejte
நல்வரவு
Mae un iaith byth yn ddigon
Bem vindo
Puô ê nnwe ga e nke e lekana,
يحتاج الأمر أكثر من لغة واحدة لتحكي قصة
مرحبًا
لا تكفي لغة واحدة أبدًا
مرحبًا
Takulandirani.

[19]

Ongi etorri.
物語を伝えるのは複数の言語がいります。
歓迎。
一つの言語は決して十分ではありません。
One langwidge ain't nuffink like innuf
cummin and av a cuppa
Eine Geschichte braucht mehr als eine Sprache.

benvenuto
ہمارے پتان کے لئے کیا سے زیادہ زبان لیتا ہے۔
Una sola lingua non è mai abbastanza.
Memakai
Velkommen
Dobra Dosli
Mirësevjen
Welkom
Wan patter is naer enough.

Wolkom
Welcome.
Fàilte
C'mon ben the hoose.
Come join our brilliant gathering.

Welcome Wee One

O ma darlin wee one
At last you are here in the wurld
And wi' aa your wisdom
Your een bricht as the stars,
You've filled this hoose with licht,
Yer trusty wee haun, your globe o' a heid,
My cherished yin, my hert's ain!

O ma darlin wee one
The hale wurld welcomes ye:
The mune glowes; the hearth wairms.
Let your life hae luck, health, charm,
Ye are my bonny blessed bairn,
My small miraculous gift.
I never kent luve like this.

Nell Ten Minutes After She Was Born

(after the photograph by Richard Greenhill, 1976)

Ten minutes after you were born,
the books fell to the one side;
your big brother continued playing Lego,
putting the bits together, as if there was an order to life,
and she stitched me up, that lovely midwife,
and sorted out my afterbirth: and cut the cord with a sharp knife.

The room was the same old, kind, mess;
clothes here, kids' books there, real life,
crumpled sheets, and on my face, sunlight. I felt
a kind of grace, a sort of embrace, an end to this strife.
The room took you in. Ten minutes later, you were my life.
Out, my little girl – out from my small room of womb, Nell.
Little Nell, our curious girl. And healthy! And well!

High Womb

After the birth (and the birth of the beautiful purple placenta,
and my joke about puff-pastry-placenta-pie, and Blossom,
the Jamaican midwife, nonplussed, struggling, *Well, then supposed*
to be good for you, full of iron, so I hear). Torn asunder.
After my beautiful boy was born blue, and put under
the grill, sunken skull – forceps – misshapen,
dark hood of head, pointed: dented.
After the long labour – *why not come out sooner?* –
I had a *high womb* for days and days and days.

My body a rough landscape; I thought of high places,
mountain ranges, remote summits, *Wuthering Heights*,
I couldn't give it up, let go – come back down.
I was a mountain goat. I lay down, legs flopped,
in the white room, withdrawn, my head elsewhere.
I couldn't see my feet for my high womb,
I couldn't see the wood for the trees.
There, there, I patted the slack, stretched skin.
There, there, baby. There, there, bonny bairn.

Pas de Deux

Would you take haud o' me,
     Take haud o' me
Haud me in your airms an' birl me aroon?
     Would you haud close tae me
      Haud close tae me
Lift me up an' put me doon?

I'll let go o' you,
Let go o' you
Turn you roon an' set you free
You're one step away
Two away frae me
A pas de chat, a pas de deux.

Would you run aff wi me
      Run awa wi me
Tak my haunds and lead me astray?
     Would you hae a word wi me,
      Hae a word wi me,
Tell me: yesterday's no the day?

I'll keep time wey you,
Bide close tae you
Yer body's memory, fu o' story,
Step by step we go – chassé, plié . . .
In your foot, your toe:
You're a magnificent glory.

Would you please follow me?
            Still shadow me
Until night becomes day?
        Keep up wi me
                Pas marché or brisé volé?
Until the river meets the sea?

I'll pace time with you,
Keep faith with you
Up the banks an' over the brae
Until the moon draps tae the sea.
I'll be your bridge, your gateway
Till you are me an' I am ye.

            Would you let go o' me,
                    Things have sapped an' ebbed away.
                        Would you let go o' me,
            Let go o' me
                    Words have slid back tae sea.
                        Who are ye? Who's me? Who's me?

I'll dance the night away
Step by step away
You go; I'll follow
Don't worry now: don't go away.
It all begins and ends with a demi-plié!
Till I am you and you are me!

Are you dancing, you say; you say
          Are you tomorrow?
        Are you asking – what will you borrow?
The day just yesterday.
            The night's dancing into the day.
The moon's dancing into the sea.

Margaret's Moon

After she died, I swear the sky
Had the most beautiful of all sunsets,
A blush of pink, then red, a glass of red,
Sudden dark and a hammock moon,
Then its faint silhouette, almost secret.
Life half-written, half unsaid.
I had kissed your head in the strange room.
Then later, I blew a kiss to the stars, to regret.

Margaret,

I imagined you lifting your head, your arms,
Loosening them, shedding skin and cells and bone
Till you became all spirit, released
Into the cairns, hills, the braes, barley,
The sea lochs and the sea and at last,
At least it seemed to me, you were free.

Is It Christmas?

(i.m. Margaret Perumal)

I wrote myself a Post-it Note.
Stuck it somewhere I forgot.
The moons came and the suns slid.
The names for things came, then hid.
Pavement, wood, boardwalk. I thought
there are certain people that talk, talk, talk.
April, September, November
But they don't mean an awful lot.
I started to taste words on my tongue:
Remember Jackie, don't lose the head.
But I still didn't find my Post-it Note.
April, September, November
Words astray, my dear heart.
It got my goat. I got upset.
But everything was OK really.
Everything is going to be OK, I say.
Are you happy? Sometimes I feel
as happy as a flower that
comes in the spring, a snowdrop.
Why snowdrops in spring? Very funny.
My mind floats like a boat downriver –
I want to gather things together.
Photographs, letters, notes. Fetch.
They jump round the house. A sair fecht.
Springing up like flowers, Post-it Notes.

Winged birds. Waded waters, things forgot.
I don't know what — gaps form the walls
April, September, November.
December: the ivy comes, sharp, spiky,
glossy, bossy, green with envy.
They envy me. They do.
And then rains come. There's Lent.
Easter, spring, summer, winter . . .
I have my money in my thick purse.
And a nice lady takes me to the sea's side
And somebody puts an ice cream into my hand.
Don't forget to flush the toilet.
The music is playing, the horses going
up and down. The past is coming
up close, like the sea in waves.
It's November, a man says.
Doesn't the year just hurtle on
slip and slide away, the lady says.
November, Mum! November,
the lady says with a funny smile.
Doesn't it just gallop along? The seahorses ran
the length of the beach.
You've scrubbed up well, I tell her; she laughs.
I find the yellow paper. I forget what it means.
Remember Jackie it says. Don't lose
the head. The sea is very far out.
And before I know
What is what, the world crashes; rushes,
November and December, Through the buildings
and doors and streets. Water. The sky fills with

smashed-up stars and tiny lights line the streets.
Bright things hang on trees, very pretty. Are
you happy? I'm happy. Are you? Somebody says
Merry Christmas. Somebody else says Merry
Christmas, Merry Christmas Mum! A glass clinks.
Spangle. Tinkle. Very funny, really. *Is it Christmas*
I hear a voice say. Oh my oh my, oh my Oh my,
Oh my, Oh my. Oh my, oh my! Oh my. My. My.

Silver Moon

How you grew up reading nights to dawn.
Books you found only here, the then unknowns:
Audre Lorde, Nikki Giovanni, Toni Cade Bambara
The Bluest Eye held up an odd mirror, Pecola Breedlove.

Switched lights on; eyes wide open – *Sula, Corregidora*
You read and read with wonder: *We Are Everywhere*:
Writings About Lesbian Parents! Or *A Raisin in the Sun*.
Voices from Women's Liberation, Maya, Djuna, Zora,

The Spinster and Her Enemies! Or Lucille Clifton.
And by the silvery light of the bookshop you grew up
By the open door, standing alone, together,
Other readers as engrossed, browsing, basking –

The blessed benevolence, the sweet, sweet ambience
Of independent bookshops, remember Thin's!
Look how you still love their names: *Voltaire and Rousseau*,
Grassroots, books gathering and honing your years:

Black and white striped spines, tiny irons, Viragos, Shebas,
The distinct spiral on the cover of your old *Bell Jar*
Your skin's pages; your heart's ink, your brain's Word Power,
Jamaica Kincaid, Bessie Head, Claribel Alegría

Don't let them turn the lights out, dears:
Keep them safe, *New Beacons*, shining stars.

Hereafter Julia

(i.m. Julia Darling)

Dear Julia, I am not yet sold on the hereafter,
Though your presence would be enough to sway me, upward.
Over the woods, tops of trees, the heavy clouds.
If there were such a place I can guarantee
It would be your radiant face I'd want to see.
Your brilliant company that'd be sought after
In the blossomy bosom of the hallowed hereafter.
There we'd be, hearing faraway Holiday.
Splitting our sides, heaving with laughter.
Sugaring a strawberry. The trees, budding, the flame leaves.
To hang out with Julia! I can see why some believe –
Why some, when stricken, want to take their leave.

Why – even dead, Julia, you're still the life and soul.
Not beleaguered. Not serious. Not too revered.

In the Long Run

Glasgow – gallus, glitzy, fu o' grace. This city's
Heartbeat's your own. Art in its DNA. No self-pity.

You'll stride across the Clyde at least twice,
Or race with your grief keeping pace alongside –

Run to meet the daughter you lost,
The father you're trying to save; your raised bet; the cost.

You'll limber up, keep on, your body a crane,
Ingenious, strong: *breathe in*, dear green place; carry on.

Aye, you'll run: fast, slow, fast, and in slow motion –
Loping past your broken heart, the ways you were mistaken

Floating like steamers on the Clyde. The past is tomorrow.
You keep going, and when you get a chance to say it, you borrow

From your other tongue – GOMA. Briggait. Gaelic, Urdu, Igbo.
Music plays inside, rising, falling: your body's The Armadillo.

Gaun yersel!

My Pitch

(Arthur Wharton was the world's first black professional footballer)

Let Arthur Wharton come back from the dead
To see the man in black blow the final whistle.
Let the game of two halves be beautiful instead,
Not years ahead. Let every kissing of the badge,
Every cultured pass, every lad and lass,
Every uttered thought, every chant and rant,
Every strip and stripe – be free of it.

Then football would have truly played a blinder,
And Arthur returned to something kinder.
Let the man in black call time on all this.
And Arthur will sing out on the wings,
Our presiding spirit – the first black blade.
Imagine having everything to play for.
This is our pitch. Now hear us roar.

Matthew's Word

This place to be named for those held and lost,
Those who were driven from their homes or fled,
For those of us not allowed to cross
The border, who might visit for an hour at most
The sacred place, if sick, if we possess a pass,
Named for those shunted from pillar to post,
Sickened by sewage, waste and rot.
No fresh water here. Electricity costly.
The land aches; the mountains roar.
Upon the hills we villagers gather at dusk
To discuss the News, circulate the word,
Weary of seeing and hearing: road blocks; check points;
Of being asked our names over again.

In the dawn light, time has ringed the years
Scored our faces; lost years, gone now.
The land is rugged in places we can't cultivate,
Mines we can't mine, quarries we can't quarry.
We hurry down the winding path to sorrow
To face the daily human failings, the distrust.
Our children learn some English words first.
Yes; please; thank you; I am not a terrorist.
Tonight, we'll gather to hear of a visit a tourist
Made to the holy land, a place as far from us
As dead sea salts, as close as the new road
We can't walk upon. We wait upon the young man
Name of Matthew's word, eager for news of our homeland.

In the early evening before we break our bread
We watch the sun sink in the V of the valley,
We listen to the call for prayer, and then pray:
Pray for years, pray for unmapped villages – no wall.
Tonight, the moon's face is marbled, the hole
In the salty lake fabled, the stars, In the locked sky, jangled.
Tonight, a father will pass a key to a son who will
Turn; give it to a mother, who will hand it to her daughter.
This is the key to our home. Call out a name;
Gather another who will do the same. Mutatis Mutandis.
Mavi Marmara. Can we forget? Can we remember?

The Ardtornish Quartet

1. Rose Cottage

My mother carried me in a cottage
Like this, sleeping on her side,
Her face turned to the wall.
Travelling spoons hanging in the dark hall.
Solace in the spill of yellow fields
In the morning, heart heavy at night.
But, day broke; waters broke – oh, the light.

Tonight, outside this Rose Cottage,
I shine my torch to watch the river
Rush as if to meet a lover, dark as the past.
In the morning I open the blinds, back at last,
And there's my river running still.
Relief. It hurries on: nobody's will.
The years are somehow carried over.

2. Lochaline Stores

Nothing can be hidden from Lochaline Stores,
Supposing the Grocer's has eyes and ears:
Not an addiction to scratch cards or whisky,
Not a partiality to a bottle of Chianti.
Not a dicky heart, not an icky stomach,
Not a forty-day habit, not a weakness for crumpets,
Not the book of first-class stamps for your love letters
Not you turning back from margarine to butter
Not a stain on your laundry – coffee, wine? –
Not your shaky I'm fine to the daily how are you?
Not your lucky-dip lottery every Saturday,
Not you, stood there in a quandary
At the sorry not this time, sotto voce.
Not the tenner on diesel, not the Wagon Wheels.
Not your last-minute rush on a Sunday,
Nor your good intention to visit Iona, one day.
Not your empty Calor gas canister,
Not your words to the fly wee Minister.
Not your face when you're low on fuel,
Not your last fiver on fishing tackle.
Not your gin, not your tonic, your wee brandy.
Not you when you're flushed, when you're peely-wally,
When the last ferry to Mull has left the jetty.
Don't get upset, don't you fret, eh? –
When you're out of sorts, you can depend on

Lochaline Stores to ken your innermost thoughts.
Don't underestimate the empathetic store:
Not only retail therapy for the terminally bored
And the terribly lonely (if a wee bit pricey) but psychoanalysis
For those whom shopping sends into total and utter paralysis!
The ones who came for a bunch of fresh parsley,
And a tin of Ambrosia creamed rice.
Or the ones who weren't sure really
What they wanted (something nice!)
Who say, when just through the door,
Not sure what I came in for . . .
When what they wanted was something more:
A small bit talk for the short days, long nights.
Safe home, safe home would even suffice.

And then it's the windy drive back,
Through the proud pines,
Over the uncertain cattle grid,
Past the empty passing places,
Where you missed your chances,
Avoiding the deer, the sheep, the stags,
The odd romances. And it's round
The bend, now, and into the dark.

3. Ardtornish Dark

Across the dark waters of Loch Aline,
small lights fluttering
from Lochaline Stores, perhaps, or the Hotel
where Charles sometimes pours a beer
and watches old westerns set elsewhere.
Or maybe from the small row of houses
(in the yellow one, Barbara lives with Arra)
that has a street lamp,
one that shines extra boldly as if to say
No many o' me here. In the distance
The odd car's headlights flicker through
black trees; still as winter, they suddenly shimmer,
lit for a moment, then back to the dark.
Here, on the other side, across the water
the light is leaving the sky, pink and blushing,
like a slow ballet dancer's last pirouette.
There's a glimmer like hope before it cools.
I walk past the fish-nets bundled like lost souls,
and head around the corner to the light
in my cottage window, left on
For myself returning, as if to company,
as if to say the lights twinkling in Loch Aline
might be a friend's Morse code from
a pink tower, or a stranger who says:
You're not alone here; you'd be more alone there.

Or, like the sound of a clock hitting the hour.
So, open your door. Get in and don't forget.
Get out the kindling; light your own fire.
Don't cheat. Don't use a firelighter.
Dance round the small room to the song.
Come on baby light my fire
Try to set the night on fire

4. Croft Near Croig

What each of us holds dear is a mystery: nostalgia.
The slabs of cheddar – the characters, Dervaig's post box.
The stories of Balfour-Paul, the myths, the seagulls
Even the railings on the ferry, the iconic ruin.

The old croft house is still practically the same old stone.
But has a new roof, and the cludgie is now a studio.
But even so, it's easy to see me back then, a girl
Putting on a show, dancing, my brother in the gods,

High up on the roof, and my mother with her bra
Straps loose, and my father too, bare-chested,
Shorts on, button undone, dark-haired, taking in the view.
And that too, unchanged, lifting the heart, now as then.

We walk in and out; stand on the new deck,
Remembering the burnt-out farmhouse years ago,
Mrs Dudgeon Brae and Sam the Shepherd, vivid as yesterday.
The late-night ceilidh, the Highland cattle at the gate

The night my mother returned home late, alone.
The goat's thin milk and the smell of the ferns.
July – the bracken, the shimmer on the bay
And the famous white sands of Calgary.

Caravan, Avielochan

The rain on the caravan roof – a skin drum, or
birds dancing – and in the morning,
the hens come to the caravan's steps, feathery feet,
on the hunt for bacon, maybe egg.
Then – guess what? BIG surprise! The period arrives!
I'm eleven. *You're eleven!* Claire Innes says.
Some don't get them till they're fourteen. Lucky you.
Don't tell your brother. Brothers are not supposed to ken.

And then, to the chemist in Aviemore, in the Morris Minor,
to get the towels mum says are like nappies.
I'm disappointed. They're nothing like nappies!
I'm all emotional. *You'll feel all emotional;*
It's natural. In the caravan, in the middle of the night,
Claire turned to me, the wee curtains shut tight,
the rain pitter-pattering the roof. *Wheesht! Wheesht!*
I went dead quiet. Not a word from me, not a word.
You've a forest there, Claire said, softly (she had no pubic hair!)
Then she pushed her tongue to the roof of my mouth –
and we kissed, we kissed, we kissed. We really did.

A Day Like Today

If every there wis a day
A doon about the mooth day,
A guy dreich and drookit day
When all ye want is tae be
Beddit under the duvet

If every there wis a day
When the hale world seemed crazy
An affy day, when ye lost the will a wee bitty,
A day when aabudy is *thon* way
Affa shivery, a Doom's day day

If every there wis a day
when the world goes frae
Bad tae wurse
Allagrugous! Lips pursed.
Cursed! in need o' a nurse!

If every a day, a day, a day
When ye didnae think you'd crack
A smile ne'er mind laugh till ye are greeting eh? Split
Sides. Laughter's a rebellion – so it is tae.
Scotland the What: the order o' the day.

It wis the day.

Beech Road Park

O but how the leaves have gone this year;
And the trees are suddenly bare.
I walk through Beech Road Park, my dear.
I thought I saw you, but you were not there.

You lost your winter scarf, my love.
And the trees lost their auburn hair.
I lost a single rust-red glove.
I thought I saw — but you were not there.

Whether you call it autumn or fall
Or the nights draw fairly in,
These are the days of little light, falling.
The deepest dark, and you can imagine.

I caught the very last of the light.
I walked fast through the small park.
I thought I saw you in the little dark.
I drew my curtains over the night.

Smith Myth

(for Ali Smith)

All the Smiths, morning to night
Night to morning, living their lives.
How special you feel being the same!
I stood on the edge of the dark waters
by the Quays. Somebody called my name.

Banished to the edge of the village,
I was the first. I dealt in fire, was fierce;
they were feart of me – blacksmith, silversmith,
but I was the wordsmith. I watched them
take flight. The clever crows, the blackbirds.

Word fluttered back home, pigeon carriers –
And if a double-decker bus crashes into us
And if the worst that could happen
Could happen to us, then we would never
Not be as strong as silver, black, gold, leather.

Nobody ever believed your name was Smith.
And we were called Smith and we lied
When we loved each other, which was true.
They thought we were making it up.
When we checked in, they laughed.

It worked for a while then it stopped.
Like love does, like a clock, hands still.
I was back at the old mills, in the dark,
Standing stock-still, listening out for the dead.
Those lives, written in the gloom.

The moon slips between the clan of red houses.
If I went as far as I could take a thing
And then turned my back, and came back in
I could be strong. Everything is paired.
Heads, tails. I nailed it. I dropped the burning coal.

There is somebody who has the gift of nobody.
In the beautiful black night at the edge of the old canal,
I could just vanish; or I could choose to live.
There is nobody who is not a somebody –
Whose heart is not open like a road.

Like the Smith's horse in the dark mooned night,
Coals still hot and smouldering.
Words hot-pressed, melding, new ones forming.
What's in a name? Everything, old friend.
The men that have taken the women's names,

The sons that have sung their mother's songs,
The small boy who said his name was everything
And the old woman who said it was nothing.
Streets and streets of heart-red,
Open arms, stranger's love, Salford.

Up around the time that I was left for dead,
I got to thinking if I had been
It would not necessarily be a bad thing.
I mean – there was me alive. Smith.
Smith. Smith. Life is a complex gift.

Care Leaver

And here's to you, brilliantly benevolent one –
For getting up each morning and getting stuff done –

For (even when things seemed tough)
Not complaining about the rough crossing –

Or the choppy waters,
Who seized the chances – lost sons, daughters;

Who'd first to search to be understood;
Who could've got lost in the underwood,

Who've given your best and then some (big nods!)
Who are our inspirations! Who intuit

The expression *carpe diem* (do it, do it!)
Who've broken from what was said, how others see them.

To you, on this day of fortune, when the leaves
Are turning, blessed oranges, reds, leaving trees.

To you who faced the bust-ups, break-ups, weight and heave.
Who cared, who took your leave. Now fill your cup!

The lights are on your face, your grace. How you turned
It around. You shine. You glow. Believe it to be so. Un-spurned.

Thinker

'An ounce of action is worth a ton of theory'
Friedrich Engels

The ground beneath our feet
may give way at any minute

so we climb to try and find
you, who hold the small key

to the brain in winter or spring,
the way reality holds imagining,

a struggle for a shorter day
when the nights come in

shifts, dusk to dawn
dawn to dusk, stars stitched —

workers are not machines
students are not consumers

we stand on your shoulders
on your acts of kindness

and you pass down this puzzle
that cannot be solved, ever:

the three great levers
heave the world out of joint

Running Water

When I left that day, you had packed my things.
You told me to take the rug and the elephants.
An act of sudden kindness, under my foot.
The winter was the summer gone wrong;
The leaves fell back to the trees, again, again

The lorry came. I forgot there was no running
water in the new hame. The road split in the rain.
Left my head in the Lantern Tree. Needed a brand-new floor.
The door: find a locksmith for the door. Loose lock.
I needed a brand-new key. Love's a bastard.

Perfume

It never worked no matter how much we loved our mothers,
or how long we left the so soft rose petals to distil — who knew? —
in glass jam jars; no matter what amount of water
we added, or how many summer nights we left it to brew;

It never worked no matter how many fresh petals to our stew
we added or took away, how often we stirred the mixture,
with our special spoon, under the full or bone moon, or left to chance:
we never came *close* to our dream perfume, our fancy fragrance.

In the end, the gift was this simple heart note:
our mother dabbed the concoction delicately onto her throat,
and behind her ears, on her wrists, sniffed, *what an aroma!*
What a lovely gift, this — she said. And we believed her. *Call it Rosa!*

Thirty-Five

As quick as you fell ill, quickly you returned;
A quip thrown back, a memory uncovered.
Saline drip, subcut, a journey undercover.
You slip into the railed bed, slide under.
Outside Glasgow Royal – snow – a thin sheet.
Inside your wit, wisdom makes my heart swell –
Bigger than your water-retaining feet.
Without this love, nothing could ever be well.
A gift the heart wrapped early in this life.
The more you give the more you will have to cherish.
If I could offer you my veins, I'd gladly use a knife.
At times, it seems if you go, I too will perish.
A mould broke, made a new mother of you.
Blood, water, sealed with a kiss: all true.

Mr Brontë's Fear Of Fire

Maybe Mr Brontë's fear of fire came earlier,
Before TB, night sweats, fever, blood-tinged sputum
Took his wife, entire kin, five daughters and a son,
Till near blind, like Rochester, and alone
He circled the table in the parlour: a lost prayer.

Perhaps Patrick Brontë could see himself like this:
Standing on the edge of a precipice,
Where a man loses everything he loves
And calls that fire, combustible destroyer, oxidizer,
No air for breath, chronic cough, a fight for air.

Maybe Mr Brontë had no word for it but fire
So – a man should fear it, the thing that runs ahead,
Consuming everything he loves, until it dawns too late:
There is no fine curtain to draw in any stone room
Between the living and the dead.

Would Jane Eyre Come to the Information Desk?

Would Jane Eyre come to the Information Desk?
The speaker voice at Heathrow Airport said.
There was I minding my own business.
And when she came near, she was shouting:
My name is Bertha; my name is not Jane Eyre
I come from Kingston, Jamaica. Look here.
Well, they'd placed handcuffs on her.
Ras! She shook her black hair and stamped
Her feet in anger: I have as much soul as you,
She was shouting to the immigration officer,
And full as much heart. My name is Bertha!
And the man was waving a form in her face
Saying sign here, sign here, Jane Eyre, sign here.
Stop shouting, dear, or you'll end up in Holding.
And Bertha was dignity – quality – know what I'm saying?
I am no bird and no net ensnares me
I am a free human being with an independent will,
She say in a voice come down from century.
Eh eh – for a minute I thought I was dreaming.
But wait! Just as suddenly as she appear
She disappear: pulled across the floor, kicking, screaming.
And a long queue instantly forming
Like a giant question across Terminal Four
And people saying the same thing. Appalling!
The way they treat that woman. Poor ting.
Who was she? Who was Jane Eyre? Who was Bertha?

And the Hinformation people saying over and over,
We are not at liberty to say anything.
We are NOT at liberty! Know what I'm saying?
And it's ME they accusing of paranoia! Ting ting!

Planet Farage

We closed the borders, folks, we nailed it.
No trees, no plants, no immigrants.
No foreign nurses, no doctors; we smashed it.
We took control of our affairs. No fresh air.
No birds, no bees, no HIV, no Poles, no pollen.
No pandas, no polar bears, no ice, no dice.
No rainforests, no foraging, no France.
No frogs, no golden toads, no Harlequins.
No Greens, no Brussels, no vegetarians, no lesbians,
    no vegan lesbians.
No carbon-curbed emissions, no CO_2 questions.
No lions, no tigers, no bears. No BBC picked audience.
No loony lefties, please. No politically correct classes.
No classes. No *Guardian* readers. No readers.
No emus, no EUs, no eco warriors, no euros,
No rhinos, no zebras, no burnt bras, no elephants.
We shut it down! No immigrants, no immigrants.
No recycling global-warming nutters.
Little man, little woman, the world is a dangerous place.
Now, pour me a pint, dear. Get out of my fracking face.

Constant

(for M.)

It is following you and you can't escape.
You cannot hold your head up or be happy.
You lose your confidence. You turn a corner: it is there.
You cannot step on it; make it disappear.
Dawn raids strike and you are terrified.
You are imprisoned in your own life.
Every time you go to the Home Office, there it is.
They make you feel inhuman. Every word you speak,
A complete lie. An untruth. You cannot begin
To imagine. It is always there. Constant.
It is your only companion. There is no freedom.
You can't really describe it.
It gets everywhere. It gets in your hair.
Under your arms; between your legs.
It gives you a bad taste in your mouth.
You can see it in your eyes; hear it in your voice.
It is hard to describe. It never takes a break.
When you walk away, it follows you. When you
Stay inside; it stays by your side, so quiet.
It is under your skin. It is your heartbeat.
Never leaves you be. It is you. It is me.
It will stroke your hand when you die.

Push the Week

(for P.)

If I had cash, I could get some cassava gari
Down Great Western Road, shop in Solly's
And make some sukuma wiki; stretch the week.
But this card don't buy me African food
Or let me shop in Marie Curie
(although they have nice things in there).
Only in the Salvation Army Store.
(Where the clothes are a bit of a bore.)
You think just because you're an asylum seeker
You don't care what you wear?
And from eating the wrong food, my stomach's sore.
If I didn't just have this card to use
I would buy some maize meal flour, avocado, yam.
If my mother were here she would say:
That woman is not my daughter.
If I had cash I could buy some corn pones,
Dried fish, beef . . . curried mung beans . . .
Kachumbari, my God, how I wish!
Expand the chest. My spirits would lift, eh?
Ugali would make me less depressed!
Not so homesick. Nyama choma.
No cash for cane row, no Makimo,
For monthlies, for sweet potato.
The week repeats. We are scattered families.
Now it's HIV. No TV. Just CCTV – watching me.

Non-stop scrutiny. Anyone shouts *Asylum Seeker*
Bash them with your saucepan. Man stealer!
(I have yet to see one to write home about!) *Cassava!*
In your imagination, you have new friends to dinner.
You picture a cooker. A table. You light a candle.
You shine some cutlery. You see your face in it.
And you say *Stick in till you stick oot*, and you say,
Help yourself. Go ahead. Have some chapati, mbazi, gari.
Here's what we eat in my country. You see.

Moss Side Mirrors

Past Roy's jerky chicken. Past Afro World, Ultra Sheen,
Sof'nFree, Dark and Lovely; the mirrored worlds between.
Past the fresh veg: yam, sweet potato, mango, plantain.
Past the fresh fish, eyes still bright and staring.

Dive in. The old roof's piano keys – big teeth, ivory.
You're an albatross. The water holds you, body and memory.
Ella, she says, put your face in the water. Learn to swim at sixty.
You put your faith in the water. It held you like a baby.

Underwater: it's another you who swims this old pool.
A mermaid, selkie – part real, part myth. Flip. Heads, tails.
You push off, float, rise. Surprise! There you are.
For a minute you don't know where you are.

The mirror in Moss Side takes all of you in
Throws you back dancing into the room.
You catch the reflection of your half-imagined twin
She's stepping out of herself into free-thinking.

Make it funky. Move to the left, to the right.
You feel your body become movement, light.
You're dancing with strangers, with total familiars.
The mirror holds the story of your days and nights.

Here's Joy, seventy-year-old Jamaican-Mancunian,
Switch! She's striding the road to the mountain.
Nice big steps. When she steps she dreams.
A girl-self glimmers; in the silver glass, gleams.

Dancing takes her to places she's never been.
The way life, with two things at once, keeps time.
I was thirty-five-years married, the woman says, through steam.
What a long sentence; I managed seven, says her companion.

Blood is pumping; the broken heart mends.
This is how we get further out. Breathe in.
Drop your tail bone. Press your head down.
Breathe out with your new-found friends.

Here you are: Jude, stamina swimmer, 64 lengths,
Girl who loves yoga, women all over, playing to strengths.
Poland, Pakistan, China, Ghana, Russia . . .
Greece, Kenya, Somalia, Georgia, India

Let me see some power! 3, 2, 1, let's go!
Young, old, in-between, no fear, no favour.
Nobody judges: some pacy, some laboured.
Some non-stop, some go-slow. Some keep time, some so-so.

Some huff and puff. Had enough. Some don't drop a bead.
Some women are ultra-fit. Some are on it!
France, Vietnam, Japan, Yemen, Ireland, Pakistan.
The young Muslim woman, hijab on, lifts you on her back.

You use each other to maintain equilibrium.
You go for a swim, steam, the age of aquarium.
A woman comes straight from her Church service
To the steam room. A hymn to steam!

A prayer for letting it all out. The body's a temple.
She's been coming to Moss Side for forty years, gently does it.
And big Lennie often rubs fresh aloe vera onto her skin.
Never go to steam without your unguents and keep your sandals on!

And here's the eighty-year-old, fiddle-fit, tuned. Samba lover.
There's a glimmer of a swagger. Can we make it bigger?
The smile of a doppelganger, we're standing tall.
Euphoria's in the air. Let it out. Roar! Say it all.

Everybody's paired with a familiar stranger.
With a long-lost self in the mirror. Come to the centre.
Lift up! Deep breath, roll those shoulders.
This is the way of the world: things you hoard, grieve over

Can just give way – accede, comply.
Gravity will help you come down. A forgotten fury.
Six-and-a-half minutes without stopping! Breathe deeply.
Stretch that spine. Here you all are, taking in the oxygen.

Here's Olivia shouting instructions! Come on! Follow your twin.
She's not resting. She's keeping time. Alone.
Olivia who told you she used to weigh fifteen stone
Till she started to dance, and the weight fell off like dead wood,

Now you wind down, slowly, slowly, take your time, understood,
Till you meet yourself coming back,
That girl, who thought much more was at stake,
That things you cared for would always break,

Who took fragile steps till she learnt to like the night.
Deep breath. You take a long look in the mirror.
There you are glowing, old, in the original light.
Moss Side has a soul. You see it shining, bright.

My Grandmother's Hair

My grandmother, Margaret, née Baxter,
had very long golden hair –
so long she could sit on it at sixteen.
She was the eldest of nine.
Her father Di Baxter
was a sot and once got picked up
drunk by the coal lorry
and dropped home with the coal.
A right character!
When her mother died young,
she walked all the way to Alloa
and all the way back
her long hair, loose with grief.
When she was ninety-one and a half
her hair was short, demi-permed, white.
She washed with cold water.
And she touched her toes
100 times a day till late in the day,
near ninety, and only stopped
jogging around the block
when she was eighty.
Never the same though
as running as a girl
her long hair flying everywhere.
In her early twenties,
she started to plait her hair into thick
braids and when she was forty

she emigrated to New Zealand.
And when she was sixty
she had the braids done
in a coil at the side of her head.
What was it called, that hairstyle?
Maybe it looked a bit severe.
(She never went in for the beehive
Or the bouffant or the poodle cut.)
In her seventies
she was taken into Sunnyside.
What did she have then – fishtails braids?
Not in your life. A bubble cut.
It was basketball hoops at 6 am
and weaving baskets for charity back then,
and when she came out of Sunnyside
(never heard a less apt name in her life –
the things she'd seen, the things she'd heard!)
she wanted back home to Scotland,
away from Christchurch and home to die.
The first time I remember meeting
my small grandmother
I was sixteen myself
fascinated by her false
teeth talking to themselves
in a glass of warm water, as she slept
and by her stories, her nightmares:
my grandfather buried alive
in the pit in Lochgelly, twice
and this part of the family speaking
to each other and these yins not,

and it was all tangled and matted
together by then, woven, unwoven,
combed, uncombed, plaited, unplaited
and as she slept in her single bed, her hair
unravelling over time, across the years
of buns and perms, pony tails and blow dryers,
her memories tumbling, falling – not Carmen Vintage
heated rollers, not the polka-dot rain cap bonnet,
not even the see-through rain-mate or the shower cap
or the hair net was ever enough
to keep it in: and finally, in the winter of
Nineteen ninety-nine, it all came out.

The Imaginary Road

The road that was in your head
Has already found you walking:
When you looked up ahead,
It was your footsteps waiting.

Then you heard the song of the road,
Under the dirt and the dust,
Heard the song of the Delta blue
And found a song you already knew.

There are roads there in the beginning;
Roads that take us to the end.
Roads we can't help loving —
The dips, turns and bends.

There's something about you now —
Small figure walking the track,
Growing into the distance
Avoiding the dips and the cracks,

Trying not to look back.
The road that was in your head
The road that was in your head
Is already up ahead.

The road that was your friend
Will be waiting in the end.
It will hold out a helping hand
As you draw your line in the sand.

ACKNOWLEDGEMENTS

Some of these poems have been published in *The Empathetic Store*, published by Mariscat Press, and others in the *Guardian*, the *Glasgow Herald*, the *Scotsman*, the *Oban Times* or broadcast on BBC Radio 3 or 4.

Thank you to the Ardtornish Estate and the Scottish Book Trust for providing me with a residency at Rose Cottage where I wrote some of these poems, to the Brontë Museum for the residency that inspired others and to the Colonsay Literature Festival.

'Lines for Kilmarnock' was written for Pidgin Perfect for a public realm space to commemorate those whose lives were changed by the First World War. 'Private Joseph Kay' was commissioned by Lives of the First World War and made into a short film of the same name by Matt Kay. 'By Accident' was written for HOME's exhibition on *Imitation of Life*. 'April Sunshine' was first a song for the London Sinfonietta and composed by Colin Matthews. 'Rannoch Loop' was commissioned by the BBC *One Show*. 'Threshold' was written for the opening of the Scottish Parliament in 2016. 'Welcome Wee One' was for First Minister's Essential Baby Box pilot. Some of these poems were responses to works in the *Tread Softly* exhibition at Yorkshire Sculpture Park. 'Pas de Deux' was commissioned by Scottish Ballet and made into a short film by Eve McConnachie called *Haud Close Tae Me*. 'Is it Christmas?' was first on Radio 3's *The Verb*. 'Hereafter Julia' is a poem written on the tenth anniversary of the death of the poet Julia Darling, commissioned for the project *Poetry Prescription* (NCLA). 'In the Long Run' was inspired by The Great Scottish Run for the Glasgow Marathon and 'My Pitch' was written for Sheffield United and Off the Shelf Literature Festival. 'A Day Like Today' was for project *Double Exposure*; 'The Imaginary Road' was a song for the musician Adam Fairhall and jointly commissioned by Manchester Jazz Festival and Manchester Literature Festival. 'Smith Myth' was commissioned by The Lowry Theatre. Some of these poems were written specially for Salford University: 'Thinker' was commissioned by curator Lindsay Taylor to sit alongside a statue of Engels' beard by the artist Jai Redman. 'Thirty-Five' was commissioned by the RSL and published in *On Shakespeare's Sonnets* (The Arden Shakespeare). 'Constant' and 'Push the Week' were written to tell the story of two Scottish refugees, and aided by the Scottish Refugee Council and the Scottish Book Trust. 'Moss Side Mirrors' was written for a Radio 4 documentary on Moss Side Leisure Centre.